Write It on Your Heart
Random Acts of Kindness Journal

Write It on Your Heart
Random Acts of Kindness Journal

From Your Friends in Unity

Edited by Rev. Ellen Debenport

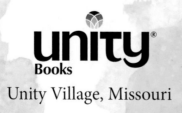

Unity Village, Missouri

Write It on Your Heart

First Edition

Unity Books are available at special discounts for bulk purchases for study groups, book clubs, sales promotions, book signings, or fund-raising. To place an order, call the Unity Customer Care Department at 816-251-3571 or email *wholesaleaccts@unityonline.org*.

Cover design: Laura Carl
Interior design: Laura Carl, Kyle Stephan, Hailee Pavey

ISBN: 978-0-87159-383-2
Canada BN 13252 0933 RT

Table of Contents

FOREWORD

What does our world need now more than ever?

Love?

Kindness?

Charitable acts?

It needs compassion for what our fellow humans are going through.

Those of us who work here at Unity World Headquarters at Unity Village love sharing positive messages through *Daily Word* or touching lives through the Silent Unity prayer ministry. We often hear that our efforts have uplifted someone's day. We are reminded that every human has a divine core and that goodness truly prevails on our planet.

But what do we actually *do* with that knowledge? How will we show up differently if we believe all humans have value? What can we do to bring light to the world?

As this beautiful passage by David Friedman says, "We can be kind. We can take care of each other. We can remember that deep down inside we all need the same thing" (*We Can Be Kind: Healing Our World One Kindness at a Time*, Mango, 2017).

In this book, Unity employees humbly offer our ideas for acts of kindness. We've created spaces for you to journal your experiences and illustrate your thoughts. Some are simple suggestions. Others are complete stories that will fill your mind with new ways you could express kindness to others. Some of these ideas are individual acts, while others could be carried out by groups. Some you might have heard before, and others are quite inventive!

These come from our personal experiences in committing acts of kindness as well as times we received kindness from others.

Of course, acts of kindness don't have to be random—some are downright premeditated!

We invite you to try our suggestions and make up more of your own. Celebrate your successes—no matter how small your act of kindness, regardless of whether anyone ever knows what you did. Take a moment to write your thoughts and feelings.

The idea that we can commit acts of kindness has been around for a long time, as well as the idea of paying it forward by doing a kindness for someone else. However, isn't this the perfect time to remember we are all in the same boat and renew our efforts to be of service to each other?

Here are our ideas. We encourage you to share your own acts of kindness with us at *kindness@unityonline.org.*

–Your Friends in Unity

♡2

Lend a HAND

Lend a Hand

Organize meal trains for community members after surgery, childbirth, or the death of a family member.

Lend a Hand

Look for opportunities to hold doors open for people.

Lend a Hand

Walk with an elderly or slower person crossing the street so they won't be alone in the intersection if the lights change.

Lend a Hand

Add a few quarters to a parking meter that is about to expire.

Lend a Hand

If you see a parent in the grocery store parking lot struggling with a couple of kids and a full grocery cart, offer to return the cart to the store or the basket return so they won't have to leave the kids in the car unattended.

Lend a Hand

If you see someone searching for their vehicle in a parking lot, try to help them find it.

Lend a Hand

You can be nice to a frustrated cashier who is having issues with a customer, or even seek out the manager to compliment a person who is doing a good job.

Lend a Hand

Write a kind or encouraging message on a paper napkin for a frazzled restaurant server.

Lend a Hand

If someone you know has lost a parent in the past year, send a card at Mother's Day or Father's Day to let them know you are thinking of them during what might be a difficult time.

Express
APPRECIATION

Express Appreciation

Look cashiers, waitstaff, and others in service roles in the eye and say, "I appreciate you." Mean it. This can be uncomfortable until you get used to doing it but once you do, it is so easy to see in their faces the difference between "I appreciate it" and "I appreciate you."

Express Appreciation

Make a special point to thank any service person—waitstaff, store clerk, telephone operator, first responders, military personnel, or hospital personnel—for working on a holiday. They might not have had a choice, but you can let them know their service on the days when most of us are with family is noticed and appreciated.

Express Appreciation

Buy an inexpensive (or expensive, if you've got the means) bouquet of flowers and give it to a total stranger for no reason other than "I thought these might brighten your day."

Express Appreciation

Send handwritten "thank you" cards through the mail. They don't even have to be thanks for anything specific. They can say, "Thank you for being a wonderful part of my life." Taking the time to write, address, stamp, and mail a note adds to the meaning of the gift.

Express Appreciation

Back in my Youth of Unity days, we would sometimes make MOLs (messages of love, similar to valentines) for the church congregation. MOLs were coveted at YOU rallies as a way to make long-lasting friends with our peers. We wanted to bring that love to our home church as well!

We would write affirmations on small, colorful pieces of paper, decorate them with glitter and stickers, then leave them under each car's windshield wiper. It always made us feel good to share our love totally selflessly, and the congregation always appreciated it.

Express Appreciation

Our church youth group regularly recognizes first responders and hospital staff by delivering cookie trays to their locations unannounced a couple times a year. The looks of surprise from these selfless people—and the opportunity for young people to connect to their community—are priceless.

In addition, the kids deliver cold water bottles and pocket snacks (granola bars, bags of chips) to local construction crews in the summer. The kids have learned to appreciate the dedication and hard work required of labor-intensive occupations.

Pay It FORWARD

Pay It Forward

Let someone with fewer items at the grocery store go in front of you. If you're really feeling generous, once their items are rung up, ask the cashier to bag them and start checking you out—so you pay for their stuff while they go on their way.

Pay It Forward

My husband and I have guardianship of our three young grandchildren. Near Christmastime, the school called my husband to the office and handed him an envelope with a card addressed to the children. It contained a really nice note stating how much our family was loved and a $100 gift card to a choice of different restaurants. The card said for the children to take grandma and grandpa out to dinner and was signed by a secret Santa.

Pay It Forward

I frequently buy specialty coffees in drive-through lanes (Starbucks, and so on), and one of my favorite things is to pay for the person in the car behind me when I pay for my own.

I also remember to tip the staff twice—once for me and once for the person behind. I don't ever see the reaction of the person I buy the coffee for, but my random act of kindness sure gives me a lift!

Pay It Forward

I experienced this as the recipient when I found out my son's frozen custard had been paid for by the person in the drive-through lane in front of me. I paid it forward a couple weeks later by paying for the car behind me when I stopped for coffee.

Pay It Forward

While on a road trip, my husband and I found ourselves with extra tollbooth change. At a rest stop and when no one was looking, we put the money into the numerous vending machines and then walked away. We didn't stay around to watch the fun but chuckled for quite a while on the long trip home thinking about the possible reactions when those machines returned the buyers' own change to them.

Pay It Forward

At some grocery stores, a 25-cent deposit is required if you choose to use a cart, then you get the 25 cents back when the cart is returned. As I'm returning a cart, I always look for someone coming into the store and offer them my cart—at no charge to them. They even get 25 cents when they return it! It will always bring a "thank you" and a smile to their face.

GIVE

What You Can

Give What You Can

Collect all the toiletries from your hotel room and donate them to homeless shelters.

Give What You Can

Buy groceries for someone in need and deliver them saying, "I was asked to bring these to you. I'm not sure who bought them."

Give What You Can

Buy some food, sit down with a homeless person, share a meal, and have a conversation.

Give What You Can

Help pay for someone's groceries if they are short of cash or if you hear the cashier say government assistance won't cover a particular item they want.

Give What You Can

My wife and I carry a couple of the following "kits" in the back seat of our car:

- Bottled water
- Kind Bar (or equivalent)
- $5 Starbucks gift card

We tape these together and when we are stopped at an intersection where a homeless person is asking for help, we have something ready to give. We know money is helpful, too, but sitting outside all day, they might appreciate a bit of water and food. They can use the card later for a warm drink or another snack.

Share
Your
GIFTS

Share your Gifts

I was over at my best friend's house and showed her a necklace that my grandpa had recently given to me. Her eyes got wide, she smiled, ran into her bedroom, and came back with a pair of earrings that perfectly matched my new necklace—as if they had been made for each other. She said, "I've had these earrings for a little while, and now I know they must belong to you!" Her kindness showed up in spontaneous generosity and a thoughtful gift.

Share your Gifts

I had a neighbor who loved music and played the piano. In the evenings she would open her window and play this great bluegrass music. I would open my kitchen window and eavesdrop (music drop?) on her. Fast-forward 25 years, and recently a lot of us former neighbors came together at a party. We started reminiscing and, lo and behold, all the other neighbors used to open their windows and music drop as well. Who knew?

Back then, this woman would also visit nursing homes and entertain the seniors. She is now 91 years old and lives in a nursing home herself, but she is still playing and entertaining, sharing her gifts.

Share your Gifts

My mother and I once created and delivered handmade Valentine's Day cards to residents of a local nursing home.

Share Your Gifts

My youngest daughter Nichole is the social worker at a nursing home. One day I was volunteering at the nursing home when a resident came by and held up her wrist to show me her bracelet. Her name was Mary and as she gently stroked her bracelet, her eyes beamed with pride.

Mary went on her way, and I told Nichole about the encounter and how much the woman loved her bracelet. Nichole responded, "I bought it at Walmart for her. It cost me $3 and Mary gets up every morning and never forgets to put on her bracelet. She stops by my office every day just to show me she is wearing it. Whenever I would speak with her, she always wanted to look at my bracelets, so I got her one."

I asked whether Mary had any kids and Nichole said no. My daughter went on to explain some things I never considered. She said everyone's situation is different when they are in their "golden years." Some don't have children or have outlived their spouse and in many cases their children. Others may have families that relocated who don't have the financial ability to take off work and travel more than once every year or two.

"The nursing home is a place where individuals need medical care," Nichole said. "It isn't senior living where the individuals are out and about or able to go on trips. Most of my individuals have limited mobility and seldom go anywhere other than for medical care.

"The saddest are those who are starved for human conversation," she continued. "We all do our best, but with so many residents, we unfortunately don't have the time during work."

My suggestion for an act of kindness is to remember there are people who can't leave their buildings. Let us be the ones who seek them out and learn what we can do to put smiles on their faces. I asked Nichole who could volunteer, and she said each state has its own requirements (background check, and so on), but anyone who wishes to volunteer can call a nursing home and ask the administrator or social worker about the greatest needs for that facility.

I asked for volunteer opportunity examples and Nichole mentioned calling Bingo, helping with art activities, and reading a book to someone who has limited vision. She said it doesn't have to be a certain or ongoing commitment. She uses volunteers whenever they have time with the residents who have the greatest need.

Nichole said birthdays become special when someone is brought a $5 pair of slippers to unwrap, when they haven't unwrapped a single gift for many years. Imagine spending every birthday, Thanksgiving, or Christmas alone. This Christmas, my oldest daughter Amy, along with my two granddaughters, 9 and 7, decided to use this year as an opportunity to show they care. Together they shopped, wrapped, and delivered small gifts for the residents where Auntie Nichole works who didn't have a visitor. In return, they received much more than they gave.

To me, being kind is just showing someone cares. What are some ways you could express caring?

Take It
OUTSIDE

Take It Outside

A great many Unity people suggested mowing someone's grass, but one had a specific story:

A person I had worked with for many years was let go. We had not worked in the same department or even spoken much for years, but I felt moved to do something for her or at least let her know I was thinking about her.

A couple of weeks later I looked her up and dropped by her house after work, but she was not home. While there I saw the lawn was badly overgrown. I drove home, brought back my push-mower, and powered through the grass, which was at least two feet high. It took well over an hour to finish.

I don't remember how she found out what I had done—I didn't leave a note—but a couple of days later she called me. I could hear the tears in her voice as she said, "You may not have known how much you were helping me, but you did. I've been working another job and my son had been mowing my lawn for me, but he hasn't been able to lately. This meant so much."

Never underestimate how powerful even the smallest act of kindness can be. It may be a greater blessing than you think.

Take It Outside

A snowfall is a beautiful opportunity to provide acts of kindness.

Clean the snow from the windshield of a random vehicle in the parking lot and put a note under the wiper blade telling them to have a nice day. Don't sign the note.

Take It Outside

It was a cold and snowy day in January sometime in the '90s. My brother and I were in our twenties and for some strange reason we both had a midweek workday off. Mike drove a delivery van that could go anywhere in the snow. There was a crazy snowstorm that day, so we drove around all day—all over Independence and Kanas City—and helped people get unstuck in the snow.

Pushing and pulling and basically helping stranded drivers get on their way, we helped dozens of people. Most offered to pay us, and we said, "No, no, it's okay. Pass it on." It was fun and made people so very happy.

Take It Outside

My neighbor Mary is one of the elders in our neighborhood. She has been living in her home for more than 54 years.

Recently she had to go to the hospital for the flu then receive therapy in her home three times a week. Mary's driveway collected more than four inches of snow in a single weekend.

My son Liam, age 4, and I put on our winter outfits and took our shovels to Mary's driveway.

We spent the next 30 minutes shoveling her driveway, the steps, and her front porch. It was a great feeling to see Mary and her daughter wave to us and say thank you through the window. Liam said to me, "Well, Dad, that was fun! When can we come back and do it again?"

Take It Outside

My street has a community mailbox that serves about 12 homes. It's too much for me to shovel an entire sidewalk, and most people drive up to the mailboxes. Simply shoveling the snow around the mailbox area makes it safer for me and others as we get out of our cars and walk around to get our mail.

Take It Outside

I love to have flowers throughout the year, and I think most people do too. When I was young I loved giving and getting flowers on May Day every year. It has been a long time since I have gotten any. It is nice receiving them, but even nicer when they come up on their own in season.

Giving flower seed packets and flower bulbs randomly to friends and neighbors during the planting season or special events is a good way to show love for them. If we send seeds with a note of appreciation and love, it is even nicer! When the flowers come up every year, they will remember the love we shared.

Take It Outside

It was May 1—a beautiful morning to check on my gardens. The Lily of the Valley bed was filled to capacity and blooming profusely. Their fragrance made me stop and give thanks to God. "These are too beautiful NOT to share," I thought. And then it hit me. "Today is May Day! I need to give these away, but to whom?"

A few years earlier, as a part-time caregiver at a small nursing home, I'd seen the lonely and unvisited. "Maybe some May Day flowers will bring them joy," I thought. One quick call to clear it with the staff, and my mission had begun! Every jelly jar, empty glass, or random coffee mug became a vase. I'll never forget my excitement as I dropped off all the flowers in their happy little vases tied with white ribbon. I was energized, and my heart was full.

Take It Outside

Help a turtle or tortoise cross the road.

Take It Outside

If you notice litter on the ground, pick it up! At work, at school, or walk around the block and clean as you go. The kindness is for everyone who comes behind you.

TRAVELING
Mercies

Traveling Mercies

In March of 2003, my son-in-law Robert was deployed to Iraq. I flew to Savannah, Georgia, where he was stationed to drive my daughter Heidi and my toddler grandson (and grand-beagle) back home to Oregon for the duration of his deployment. It was an adventure we will always remember, especially our transit through Texas.

On the eastern border of Texas, we stopped in Beaumont for supper and rest. While finishing our meal, we asked for to-go boxes from the Chinese restaurant where we had dined. The proprietress insisted on boxing our food herself and added more boxes, more food, including a full box of almond cookies. Each time I started to protest her generosity, she waved her hand in dismissal and said, "For the baby, the baby needs this." She was such a blessing for weary souls—for days to come!

Traveling west the next day, we stopped at a rest stop in the early afternoon. As we all trooped back to the car, we noticed something under the windshield wiper on the driver's side. There was a neatly folded note that read, "Blessings on your journey," and a $20 bill tucked inside.

By the time we reached El Paso on the western border of Texas, we were all ready for a meal and rest again. We found a motel and ordered food, and my daughter volunteered to go get the order. In a new city, with fatigue starting to catch up with her, she wasn't sure how to find her way back to the motel. She returned to the restaurant for directions, and a woman told her not to worry, she would drive her car so Heidi could follow in her own vehicle back to the motel.

It was a time of tensions and worry for the entire nation back then, but these wonderful people made our time a little brighter. My son-in-law safely returned from Iraq to his growing family, and I will always wish continued blessings to those kind strangers. And, of course, God bless Texas!

ACKNOWLEDGEMENTS

Thanks to the staffers at Unity World Headquarters who contributed their ideas for random acts of kindness!

Ben Jamison
Charlotte Reynolds
Cheri Jamison
Cindy Entwistle
Collena Nattrass
Debie Cammisano
Dorothy Meier
Elaine Meyer
Ellen Debenport
Gregg L. Davis
Griseyda E. Segovia
Heidi Spease
Janelle M. Rubelee
Jerry Shipman
Julie Stofer
Kathleen Heifner
Katie Hawthorne
Kim Wheeler
Lila Herrmann
Lori Sales
Marc Evason
Marilyn Combellick
Matthew Kent
Michael Kincaid
Pamela Shaner
Patti Busse
Rhonda Peterson
Shannon Sleeper
Toni Cardarella
Veronica O'Neill

HOW MAY WE SERVE YOU?

Through prayer, publishing, and events, Unity is always here to support you in expressing your divine potential for a healthy, prosperous, and meaningful life:

PRAYER SUPPORT

Call Silent Unity® at 816-969-2000 for personal prayer anytime, day or night, or visit *silentunity.org* to submit your prayer request online.

INSPIRATIONAL PUBLICATIONS

Call 816-969-2069, Monday-Friday, 7:30 a.m.-4:30 p.m. (CT), or visit *unity.org*.

- *Daily Word®* in regular, large type, digital, or Spanish (*La Palabra Diaria*)
- *Unity Magazine®*
- Books, both in print and e-books
- CDs and DVDs

UNITY RETREATS AND EVENTS

Call 816-251-3540, Monday-Friday, 7:30 a.m.-4:30 p.m. (CT), or visit *unityvillage.org* to see detailed information for workshops, retreats, and special events.

ONLINE RESOURCES

- Articles, prayers, meditation, news, and information at *unity.org*.
- Spiritual programming 24/7 at *unityonlineradio.org*.
- *Daily Word* messages and related content at *dailyword.com*.

Unity is a 501(c)(3) nonprofit organization, supported primarily by freewill offerings, including planned giving. To give a donation, please visit *unity.org/donatenow*. Thank you in advance for your support.

–Your Friends in Unity